Aunt Matilda's Almost-Boring Party

Jane Morris Udovic

ILLUSTRATED BY

David Udovic

FRONT STREET
HONESDALE, PENNSYLVANIA

To Terry, my oh-so-perfect husband,
and in loving memory of my mother, Helen Denison Morris
—*J.M.U.*

To Susan
—*D.U.*

Text copyright © 2009 by Jane Morris Udovic
Illustrations copyright © 2009 by David Udovic
All rights reserved
Printed in China
Designed by Helen Robinson
First edition

Library of Congress Cataloging-in-Publication Data

Udovic, Jane Morris.
Aunt Matilda's almost-boring party / Jane Morris Udovic ;
illustrations by David Udovic. — 1st ed.
p. cm.
Summary: Aunt Matilda's nephew nods off at her snooty charity ball,
only to miss some very messy fun.
ISBN 978-1-59078-653-6 (hardcover : alk. paper)
[1. Stories in rhyme. 2. Balls (Parties)—Fiction. 3. Aunts—Fiction.
4. Humorous stories.] I. Udovic, David, ill. II. Title.
PZ8.3.U33Au 2009
[E]—dc22
2009001248

FRONT STREET
An Imprint of
Boyds Mills Press, Inc.
815 Church Street
Honesdale, Pennsylvania 18431

Aunt Matilda always does things
in her oh-so-perfect way.
She has planned a fancy party
and has ordered me to stay

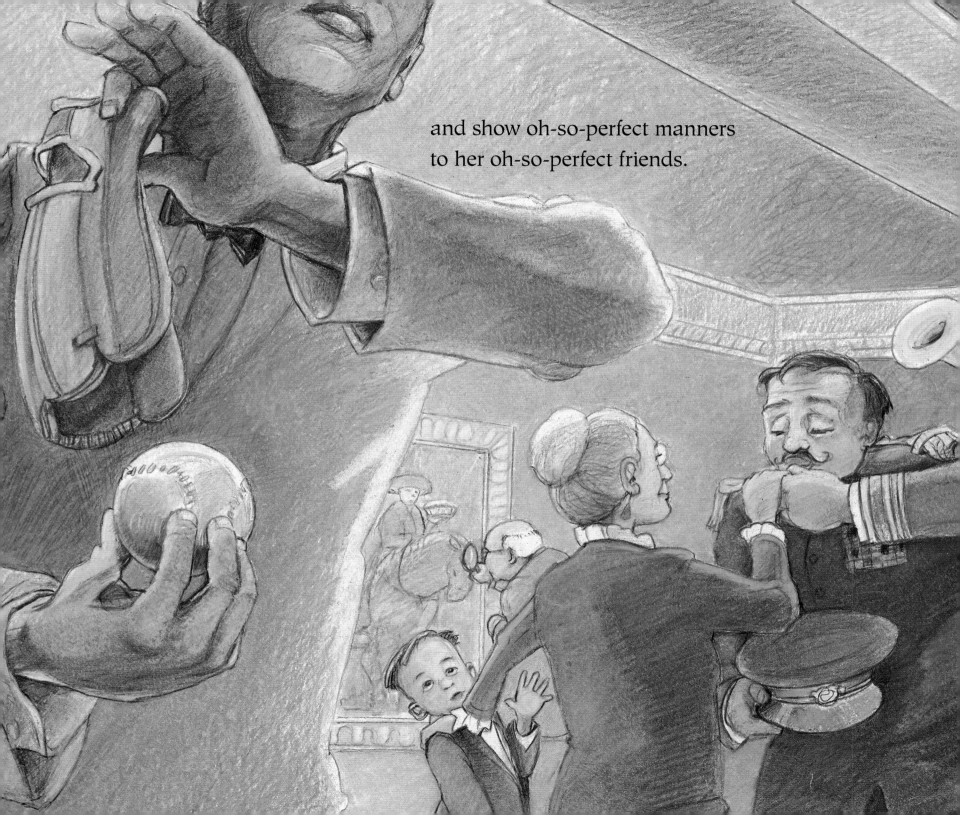

and show oh-so-perfect manners
to her oh-so-perfect friends.

But I'm sleepy and I'm bored now,
and I hope this party ends!

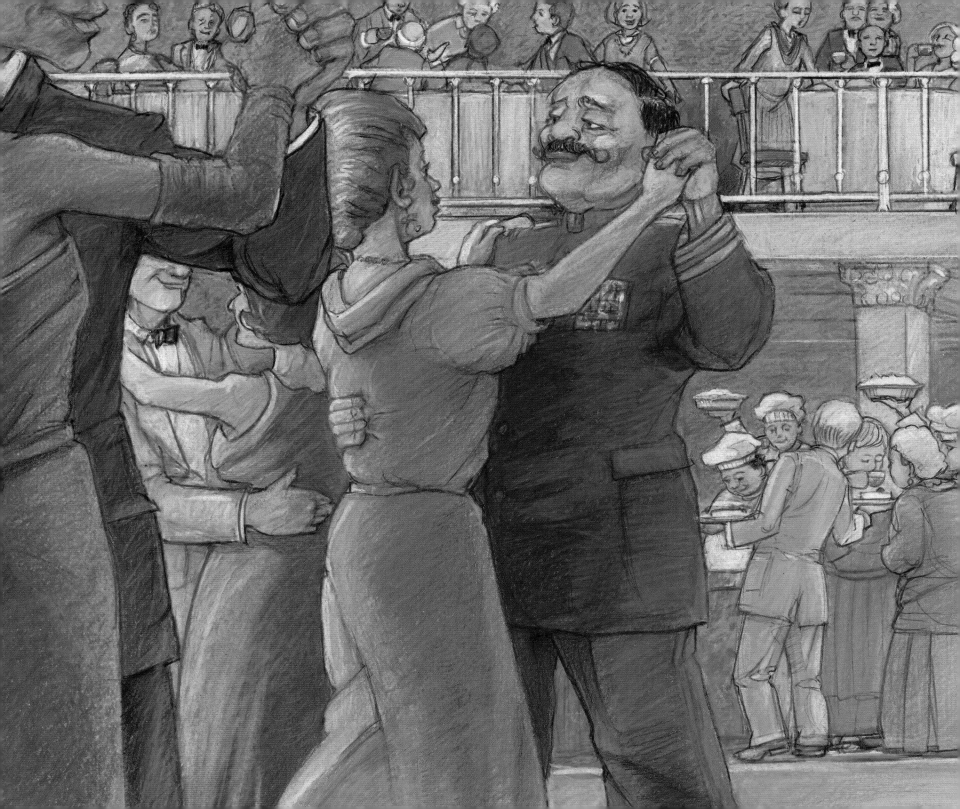

So I slouch down in an armchair.
Ahh … I try to catch a yawn.

Ohh … I feel my eyelids drooping.
Zzzzz … Then suddenly, I'm gone!

Whap! My hand slams on the corner
of a lemon custard pie.
Then it flies up, soars and twirls, and

lands ... *kerplop!* ... in Auntie's eye!

Quick! I need a spot to hide in!
Crash! The punch bowl tumbles down.
What an awful mess I'm in now!
I can feel my Auntie's frown.

I dart right, then left, escaping
from a pie that's aimed my way.

As I duck, the gooey
filling hits the
General's toupee.

Wow! My perfect Aunt Matilda's
handing out the creamy pies!

Now we swirl and whirl like dancers
as a fudge cream zooms right by.

Then we listen to the *split-splat*
as pies fly across the air.

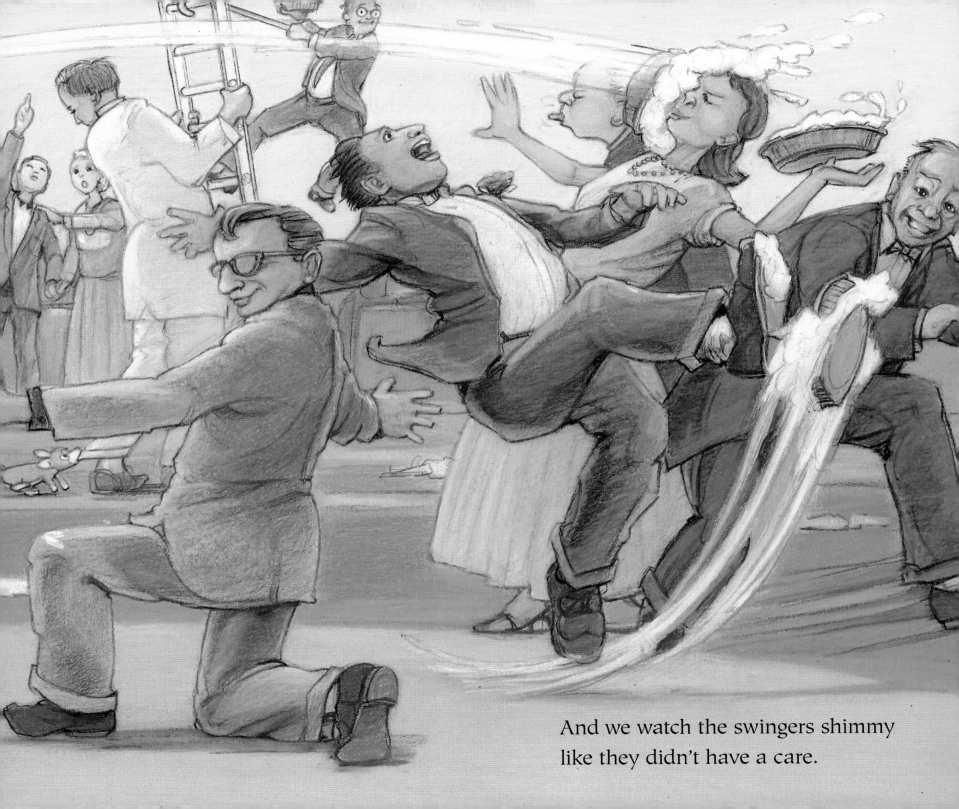

And we watch the swingers shimmy
like they didn't have a care.

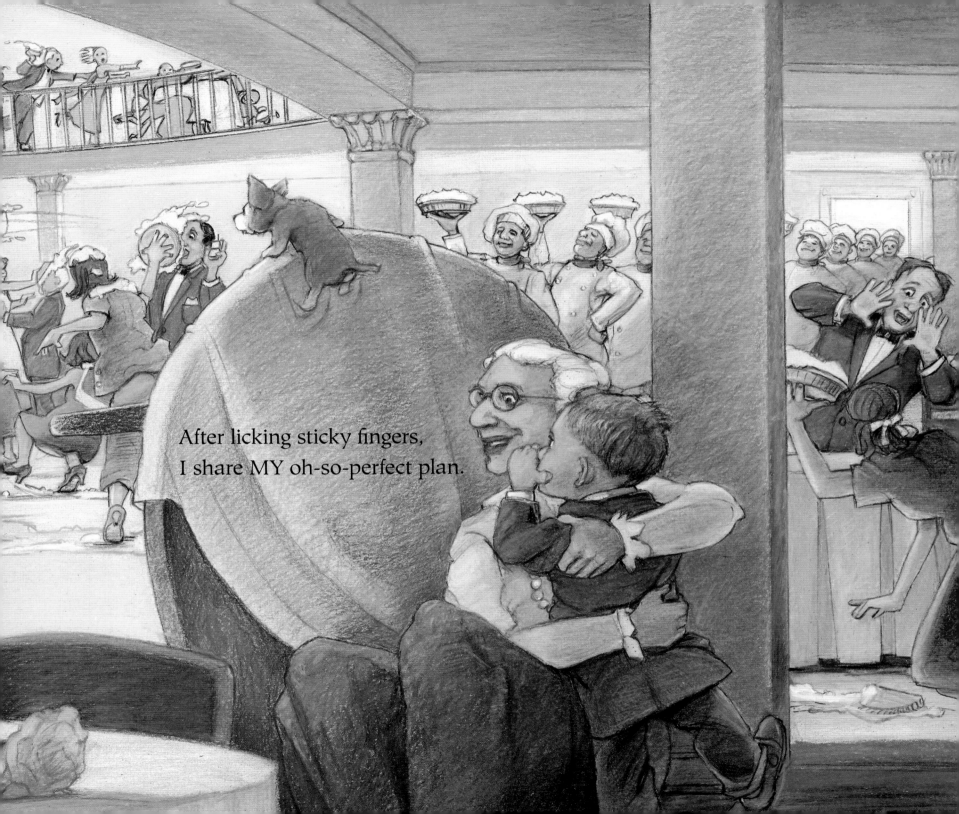

After licking sticky fingers,
I share MY oh-so-perfect plan.

"Auntie, join my BIRTHDAY BALL game.
Oh, I really hope you can!"